THE 100% UNOFFICIAL BIOGRAPHY: ONE DIRECTION 3D
A BANTAM BOOK Hardback edition 978 0 857 51336 6
Paperback edition 978 0 857 51349 6

First published in Great Britain by Bantam,
an imprint of Random House Children's Publishers UK
A Random House Group Company

This edition published 2013

10 9 8 7 6 5 4 3 2 1

With special thanks to Dan Newman at Perfect Bound Ltd.

PHOTO CREDITS Alex Emanuel Koch/Shutterstock.com: 33 (water). Atlantic Music Ltd: 30 (Sheeran). Beelover9481/cc-by-2.0: 31 (Beyonce). Beretta/Sims/Rex Features: 41tl, 48t, 55b. blue67design/Shutterstock.com: all doodles. Brian Rasic / Rex Features: 12t, 14t, 25, 26, 27, 51, 57. Broadimage/Rex Features: 11, 30 (BSB), 44m, 45m (The Wanted). Buzz Foto/Rex Features: 48b. Christopher Macsurak/cc-by-2.0: 30 (Minaj). compulsiveprep_8/cc-by-2.0: 31 (Scherzinger). Copetti/Photofab/Rex Features: 10, 41tm. Courtney/cc-by-2.0: 32 (Portman). Criii/cc-by-2.0: 31 (Lott). Crystalspman/cc-by-2.0: 32 (Coldplay). Danny Smythe/Shutterstock.com: 32 (sweetcorn). David Fisher/Rex Features: 8, 9, 13, 19, 45b (Union J), 53b, 54tl. David Jones/cc-by-2.0: 30 (McFly). DeskyCom/Shutterstock.com: 33 (snake). Eric Isselee/Shutterstock.com: 32 (lion). Erik Pendzich/Rex/Rex Features: 20t, 41tr. Everett Collection/Rex Feature: 18t. gjkooijman/cc-by-2.0: 30 (Burke). gresei/Shutterstock.com: 33 (olives). illustrart/Shutterstock.com: 32 (pizza). jaroslava V/Shutterstock.com: 32 (giraffe). Jonathan Hordle / Rex Features: 60. Julia Ivantsova/Shutterstock.com: 61 (glasses). Kevin Mazur/Getty Images: 5 & cover (singers). Layland Masuda/Shutterstock.com: 33 (sauce). lkphotographers/Shutterstock.com: 33 (spoons). London News Pictures/Rex Features: 30 (Westlife), 45t. Masatoshi Okauchi/Rex Features: 49m. Matt Baron/BEI/Rex Features: 6, 15, 16b, 32 & back cover, 41br, 46, 54bl, 54br, 55t, 61 (Zayn). McPix Ltd/Rex Features: 5 & cover (crowd). McPix/Rex Features: 16t. McPix/Rex Features: 56. MediaPunch/Rex Features: 49t. NAS CRETIVES/Shutterstock.com: 33 (fake tan). Newspix/Rex Features: 18b. Nikki To/Rex Features: 22, 49b. Nils Jorgensen/Rex Features: endpapers, 52b. oksana2010/Shutterstock.com: 32 (turtles). Olycom SPA/Rex Features: 44t. Owen Sweeney/Rex Features: 58. Perfect Bound Ltd: all paper backgrounds. Peter Dutton/cc-by-2.0: 32 (Timberlake). phloen/Shutterstock.com: 33 (beans). Picture Perfect/Rex Features: 36. PictureGroup/Rex Features: 14b. pinguino k/cc-by-2.0: 32 (Fox). PLV/NMA13/SIPA/Rex Features: 52t. Public domain (US Navy): 30 (Clarkson), 31 (Bon Jovi). Rex Features: 20b, 24, 28, 31 (Ferguson), 31 (Lewis), 31 (JLS), 32 (Lewis), 40bl, 42, 54tr, 61 (Belle Amie). Richard Young/Rex Features: 31 (Grimshaw), 31 (Corden). Rob Cable/Rex Features: 41bl. robataoo-san/cc-by-2.0: 30 (Gaga). Robyn Mackenzie/Shutterstock.com: 32 (toast). rocor/cc-by-2.0: 30 (Spears). Sara Jaye/Rex Features: 31 (Edwards), 40br. Scottish Beauty Blog/cc-by-2.0: 31 (Flack). Singhanart/Shutterstock.com: 61 (carrots). Sony Music: 31 (Murs). Startraks Photo/Rex Features: 12b, 31 (Swift), 32 (NSYNC), 34, 40tr, 44b. Unimedia Images/Rex Features: 21. Valentyn Volkov/Shutterstock.com: 33 (mayonnaise). Willi Schneider/Rex Features: 53. yukipon/Shutterstock.com: all tapes on pics.

The Random House Group Limited supports the Forest Stewardship Council® (FSC®), the leading international forest-certification organisation. Our books carrying the FSC label are printed on FSC®-certified paper. FSC is the only forest-certification scheme supported by the leading environmental organisations, including Greenpeace. Our paper procurement policy can be found at www.randomhouse.co.uk/environment.

Set in Neo and Thirsty Rough

Bantam Books are published by Random House Children's Publishers UK,
61-63 Uxbridge Road, London W5 5SA

www.randomhousechildrens.co.uk
www.randomhouse.co.uk

Addresses for companies within The Random House Group Limited can be found at:
www.randomhouse.co.uk/offices.htm

THE RANDOM HOUSE GROUP Limited Reg. No. 954009

A CIP catalogue record for this book is available from the British Library.

Printed in Italy

THE 100% **UNOFFICIAL** BIOGRAPHY

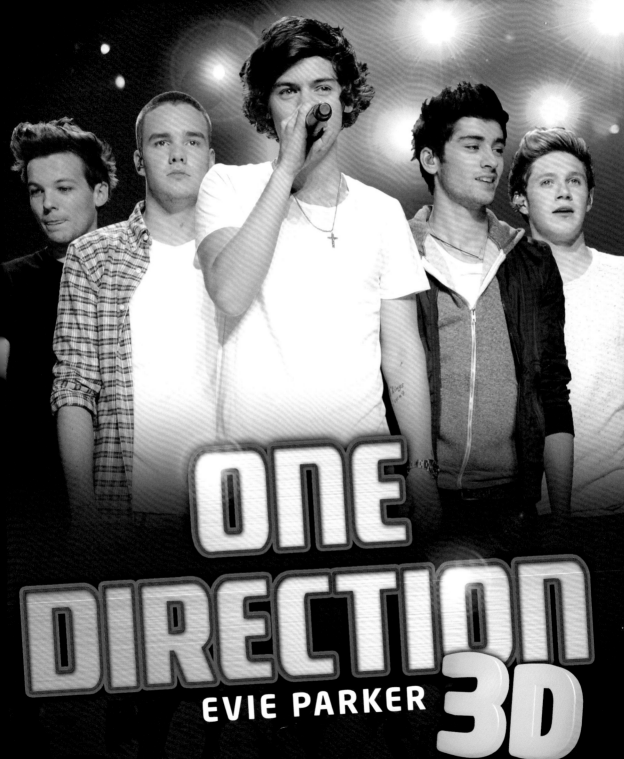

ONE DIRECTION 3D

EVIE PARKER

Contents

Page 18

Page 42

Page 52

One Amazing Story

In 2010 these five young men didn't even know each other. Now they do . . . and so does everyone else in the world!

What a result!

Liam, Louis, Zayn, Niall and Harry have been busy, haven't they? Two albums straight to number one in America – and dozens of other countries. Sell-out concerts in cities all around the globe. Massive crowds of screaming fans wherever they go. Not bad going, boys, not bad at all . . .

No guarantees

It was never *certain* that One Direction were going to make it. They could all sing well, but none of them were good enough to get to Boot Camp in *The X Factor* as solo artists. Only Niall plays an instrument on stage, and Zayn hated dancing to start with. And just because Simon Cowell told them to form a band, it didn't *guarantee* they were going to succeed.

Thanks to the fans

So why is it all turning out so well for One Direction? Firstly, the boys work so fantastically together, as a group. And secondly, their wonderful fans have supported them with passion and commitment – it's all down to you!

▼▲ Before and after the Brit Awards, February 2013: One Direction won the global success award for international sales in 2012.

9

So how did they make the leap from students to superstars? Here's a recap . . .

2010

June	Five boys audition as solo candidates for *The X Factor*. The judges are Cheryl Cole, Simon Cowell, Louis Walsh and Dannii Minogue.
July	Auditions end. The boys fail to progress to Boot Camp as solo singers, and are told to try out as a group.
Aug	They only get five weeks' practice, but Simon Cowell is really impressed with the boys and puts them through to the live show.
Oct	From the start they wow the judges – and the viewers!
Nov	Every week their *X Factor* performances get better.
Dec	The Final. One Direction sing with Robbie Williams, who backs their bid for the top spot – but they are beaten into third place by Rebecca Ferguson and Matt Cardle.
Dec	Sign a contract with Simon Cowell and Syco Records.

2011

Jan	Begin recording first album.
Feb–Apr	Perform on *The X Factor Live* tour.
May	Recording continues, in Stockholm, London and Los Angeles.
Sept	Release 'What Makes You Beautiful', which goes straight to number one in Britain.
Nov	Release their first album, *Up All Night*.
Nov	Sign with Columbia Records in America.
Dec	Start their first UK concert tour.

▲ Celebrating the end of *The X Factor*, December 2010.

10

'I didn't sit here two years ago with some master plan. We just had five brilliantly talented people who I really liked. We made the best record we could, and we hoped for the best.'

Simon Cowell

2012

Feb	Visit America as opening act for Big Time Rush, do lots of promotion work.
March	15,000 fans turn up for their first US TV appearance in New York.
Apr-Jul	Continue to tour America and Australia while also recording their second album.
Aug	Perform at the closing ceremony of the London 2012 Olympics.
Sept	Get nominated for 3 awards at the MTV Video Music Awards including Best New Artist – and win all three!
Sept	Release 'Live While We're Young', which hits top tens everywhere.
Nov	Release second album *Take Me Home*.
Dec	Perform at the Royal Variety Performance and Madison Square Garden.

2013

Feb	Release 'One Way or Another (Teenage Kicks)' as the Comic Relief single.
Feb	Begin a MASSIVE world tour . . .

▼ At the 2012 MTV Video Music Awards, Los Angeles.

11

Harry

Full name	Harry Edward Styles
Date of birth ...	1 February 1994
Home town	Holmes Chapel, Cheshire
Siblings	One older sister
Star sign	Aquarius
Height	1m 78cm
Eyes	Green
Hair	Brown (and BIG)
Twitter	@Harry_Styles

Harry was only 16 when 1D took off, and you might have thought he wouldn't cope with being famous – but mega-stardom seems to suit him pretty well. His easy charm, quick wits, good looks and winning smile have made him everybody's darling. He's got plenty of celebrity friends – his bandmates are constantly surprised at who he knows. They're not surprised to see him naked, though – Harry just loves getting his kit off!

▲ On stage in London, January 2012.

◄ Holding hands with, oh, just some girl he met .... (Yeah, Taylor Swift. We know).

Harry is famous for that fab floppy fringe. He's said he'd like to change it some day - but no-one will let him get it cut!

"I'm trying to be a bit more careful about what I do and say now, but it's really hard. We get into trouble about 5 times a day!"

Did you know?
Harry has **dozens** of tattoos all over his body. The list includes his sister's name, a pirate ship, two sparrows, an Iced Gem and a coat hanger!

13

Niall

Full name ..... Niall James Horan
Date of birth .. 13 September 1993
Home town .... Mullingar, Ireland
Siblings .... One older brother
Star sign ...... Virgo
Height 1m 70cm
Eyes .... Blue
Hair .... Dark brown
(under the dye!)
Twitter .... @NiallOfficial

Aah. Sweet, lovely Niall. No-one has a bad word to say about him, and he may actually be the most popular with the fans (at least, his doll sold more than the others in 2012). His dad describes him as a lovely, well-mannered, well brought-up lad - though he does like to swear a bit, so he tends to keep quiet in interviews to avoid blurting out a rude word! He can also let rip from the other end - bandmates reckon he's the worst trumper in One Direction!

▲ On stage in London, January 2012.

Niall suffers from somniloquy - which means he talks in his sleep. Also, he's pretty noisy when he's awake!

◀ Performing at the American *X Factor* Season Final in Los Angeles, December 2012.

14

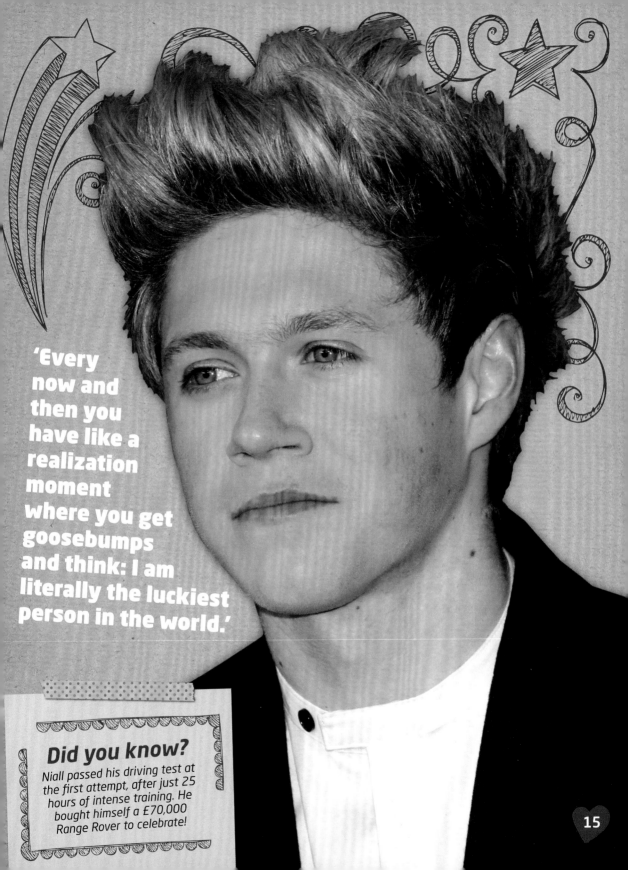

'Every now and then you have like a realization moment where you get goosebumps and think: I am literally the luckiest person in the world.'

Did you know?

Niall passed his driving test at the first attempt, after just 25 hours of intense training. He bought himself a £70,000 Range Rover to celebrate!

15

Liam

Full name . . . . . Liam James Payne
Date of birth . . 29 August 1993
Home town . . . . Wolverhampton
Siblings . . . . Two older sisters
Star sign . . . . . . Virgo
Height 1m 78cm
Eyes . . . . Brown
Hair . . . . Dark brown
Twitter . . . . @Real_Liam_Payne

Liam's not the oldest, but in some ways he's more grown up than the other lads. They call him 'Daddy Directioner', because he tries to motivate and organise them. Good luck with that, Liam!

He had a wonky kidney as a child that meant he had to be careful what he drank, and had to stay super-healthy. The kidney seems to have righted itself, luckily. He's a physical type – he reckons he's the best dancer in the band, and was a boxer at school. However he's not that lucky – the boxing led to plenty of bruises, a broken nose and a perforated eardrum. Ouch! And in 2012 he dropped a laptop on his foot and broke his toe. *Enough* with the injuries, Liam!

▲ Shaggy Liam at Louis' old school in Doncaster, December 2010.

▼ Sleek Liam (and Louis) arriving for the Brit Awards, February 2013.

16

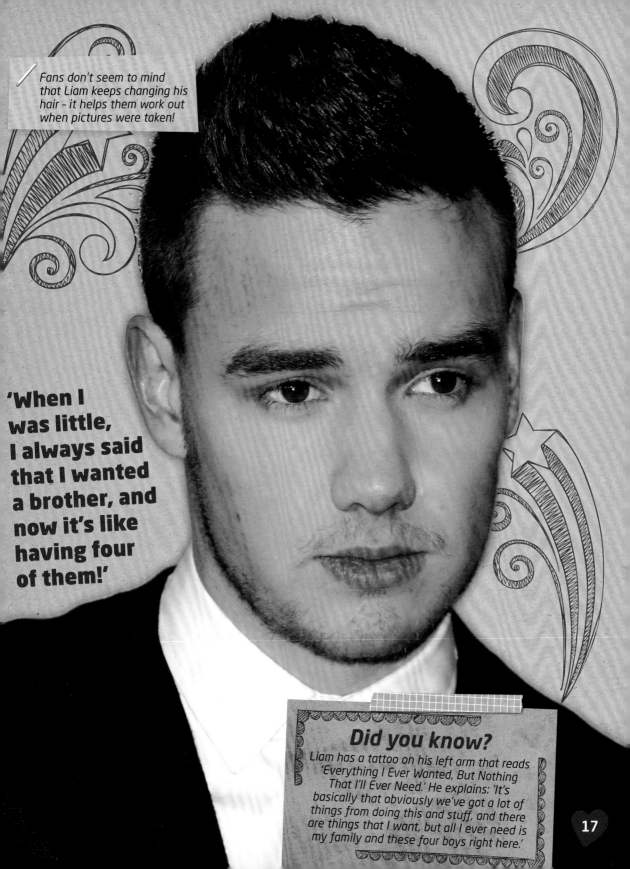

Fans don't seem to mind that Liam keeps changing his hair - it helps them work out when pictures were taken!

'When I was little, I always said that I wanted a brother, and now it's like having four of them!'

Did you know?

Liam has a tattoo on his left arm that reads 'Everything I Ever Wanted, But Nothing That I'll Ever Need.' He explains: 'It's basically that obviously we've got a lot of things from doing this and stuff, and there are things that I want, but all I ever need is my family and these four boys right here.'

17

Zayn

Full name ..... Zayn Javadd Malik
Date of birth .. 12 January 1993
Home town .... Bradford
Siblings .... Three sisters – one older, two younger
Star sign ...... Capricorn
Height 1m 75cm
Eyes .... Light brown
Hair .... Black
Twitter .... @zaynmalik

▲ Performing in New York, November 2012. Love that blond streak!

The brooding serious one . . . not really! Zayn makes the most of his dashing dark looks, pouting into the camera while the others grin and pull faces.

The phenomenal success of 1D has been a tough journey for Zayn. In 2010 he almost walked out of boot camp, because he didn't think he could dance. Simon Cowell persuaded him to keep going, and he learned soon enough – now he's always busting some wild moves!

Before *X Factor* Zayn didn't even have a passport, and had never talked or performed in front of an audience. He seems to have got the hang of it now . . .

He misses his family when he's on tour, but the support of his bandmates has helped him cope. He's annoyed that they're so messy though – he reckons he's the neatest member of the band!

▼ Zayn has said he'd wear nothing but black if he had to choose.

Zayn applied for The X Factor in 2009, but pulled out because he was too nervous to perform.

'Life's a funny thing, the minute you think you've got everything figured, something comes along and turns it all upside down.'

Did you know?

Zayn has fewer tattoos than Harry, but he got his first – and they're bigger. There's a full-size microphone on his arm and a crown on his chest, to represent his surname (which means 'king' in Arabic).

19

Louis

Full name	Louis William Tomlinson
Date of birth ..	24 December 1991
Home town	Doncaster
Siblings	Five younger half-sisters
Star sign	Capricorn
Height	1m 75cm
Eyes	Grey-blue
Hair	Brown
Twitter	@Louis_Tomlinson

He may be the oldest, but Louis can be pretty childish sometimes, and says he has no plans to grow up. He likes a prank and a laugh, especially with his best mate Harry. He's quite the fashionista – he's been seen at fashion shows, and the others say he brings the most clothes on tour. They also reckon he's the messiest, and has the smelliest feet!

Before 1D catapulted him to stardom, Louis did a bit of acting while he was at school, as well as singing in a band called The Rogue. Being world-famous hasn't changed him too much. He's still in touch with plenty of his old friends and has even invited them on tour.

▲ Looking cool in New York, November 2012.

▼ Now, what nickname could you give this pair? Louis and Harry, hmm ...

Louis doesn't want his bandmates to wear stripes. That's HIS look, right?

'We're not perfect, we're not clean cut. We're trying to be ourselves.'

Did you know?

That whole 'I love carrots' thing got pretty boring for Louis, after he kept getting given piles of orange veg. He now says he loves Lamborghinis - any luck with that yet, Louis?

21

Sounds Great!

Everything you ever wanted to know about every song the boys have recorded . . .

One Direction's journey through *The X Factor* helped them grow in confidence and skill, as they explored different song styles. They became better and better as a band and we were all super-impressed by their versatility and ability – though sadly that wasn't enough to get them to the winner's spot!

Before the final, One Direction had already recorded 'Forever Young' (from 1984, by Alphaville). This was going to be their debut single, if they won. But when they lost out to Rebecca Ferguson and Matt Cardle, the single was shelved . . .

With the other *X Factor* finalists, One Direction recorded a charity single, 'Heroes' by David Bowie, and toured Britain with *The X Factor* Live.

'Forever Young' was leaked onto the internet – where it gathered millions of hits around the world. Clearly there were plenty of fans out there!

▼ Calming the crowds in Glasgow, April 2011.

One Direction's X Factor songs

Week	Theme	Song	Artist
1	Number Ones	'Viva La Vida'	Coldplay
2	Heroes	'My Life Would Suck Without You'	Kelly Clarkson
3	Guilty Pleasures	'Nobody Knows'	Pink
4	Halloween	'Total Eclipse of the Heart'	Bonnie Tyler
5	American Anthems	'Kids in America'	Kim Wilde
6	Elton John	'The Way You Look Tonight'	Elton John
7	The Beatles	'All You Need Is Love'	The Beatles
8	Rock	'Summer of 69' 'You Are So Beautiful'	Bryan Adams Joe Cocker
9	Club Classics	'Only Girl (In The World)' 'Chasing Cars'	Rihanna Snow Patrol
10	The Final	'Your Song' 'She's the One' 'Torn'	Elton John Robbie Williams Natalie Imbruglia

The 2010 X Factor charity single was recorded in aid of Help for Heroes and reached number one in both the UK and Ireland - the first time 1D topped the charts! The boys came back for the X Factor charity single in 2011 ('Wishing on A Star' by Rose Royce, in aid of Together For Short Lives).

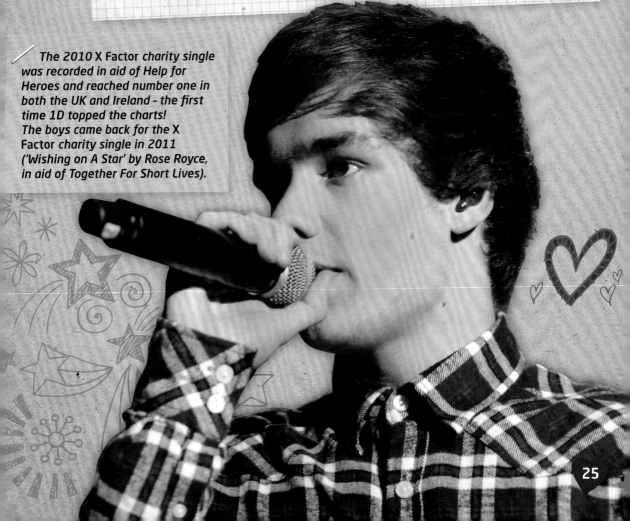

25

Sounds Great!

1D started work on their first album while they were still on *The X Factor Live* tour, and carried on over the summer of 2011, with some of the best writers and producers in the business. Their first single, 'What Makes You Beautiful', was released in September, and went straight to number one in Ireland and the UK. And from that great start, things just got better!

'What Makes You Beautiful' won the BRIT Award for Best British Single in 2012

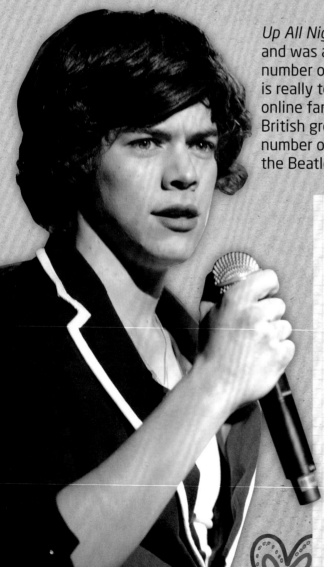

Up All Night was released in November 2011, and was a huge success everywhere - it got to number one in 16 countries! In America, this is really tough, but thanks to some amazing online fans, One Direction became the first British group **ever** to enter the US charts at number one with their debut album. Not even the Beatles managed that!

Up All Night tracklist

1   'What Makes You Beautiful'
2   'Gotta Be You'
3   'One Thing'
4   'More than This'
5   'Up All Night'
6   'I Wish'
7   'Tell Me a Lie'
8   'Taken'
9   'I Want'
10 'Everything About You'
11 'Same Mistakes'
12 'Save You Tonight'
13 'Stole My Heart'

Limited edition bonus tracks (varies)
14 'Stand Up'
15 'Moments'
16 'Another World'
17 'Na Na Na'
18 'I Should've Kissed You'

The boys toured the world in 2012, while working on their second album at the same time – which must have been really hard work. It's amazing they looked so happy most of the time! Again, some really talented people were involved – *Take Me Home* was written with the boys' singing strengths in mind, to suit their individual voices.

To show off their second album, 1D began a massive tour in February 2013 – over 100 dates all around the world. Fans were so eager to see their favourite band that tickets sold out almost everywhere as soon as they went on sale. Can't wait to see you guys!

Take Me Home reached number one in 35 countries, and was the fourth-bestselling album of 2012 in the world!

27

In 1969 The Beatles released their album Abbey Road. The cover showed the band walking across the zebra crossing in . . . you guessed it, Abbey Road! As massive Beatles fans, 1D were happy to pay their respects and be snapped doing the same move as their heroes.

Can you spot ten differences between these two pics?

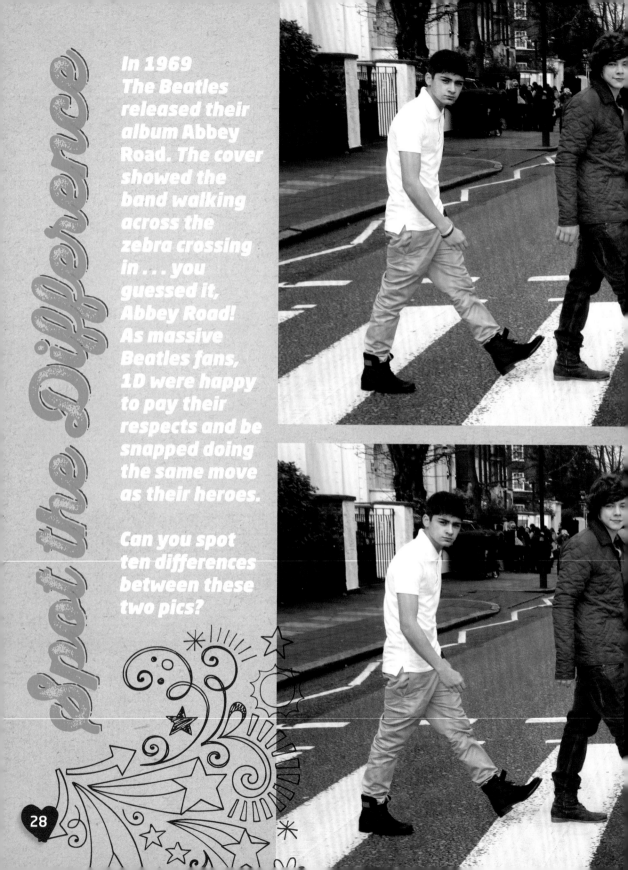

29

Celebrity Links

One Direction were lucky to meet some well-connected people right from the start!

Backstreet Boys

Kelly Clarkson

Ed Sheeran

McFly

LOUIS   **NIALL**   **LIAM**

Savan Kotecha

Carl Falk

Rami Yacoub

Alexandra Burke

Lady Gaga

Nicki Minaj

Britney Spears

Westlife

Nick Grimshaw

James Corden

Olly Murs

Caroline Flack

Rebecca Ferguson

Beyoncé

Taylor Swift

ZAYN   HARRY

Toby Gad

Steve Mac

RedOne

Pixie Lott

Leona Lewis

Perrie Edwards

Bon Jovi

Nicole Scherzinger

JLS

31

Likes and

*NSYNC
Zayn ✔

Justin Timberlake
Zayn ✔

Coldplay
Harry ✔

Leona Lewis
Liam ✔

Megan Fox
Zayn ✔

Sweetcorn
Harry ✔

Natalie Portman
Louis ✔

Pizza
Niall ✔

Marmite on toast
Louis ✔

Lions
Zayn ✔

Giraffes
Niall ✔

Turtles
Harry ✔

32

© Broadimage/Rex Features

© David Fisher/Rex Features

© Matt Baron/BEI/Rex Features

© Rex Features

© David Fisher/Rex Features

© David Fisher/Rex Features

© David Fisher/Rex Features

Dislikes

...hat they love and hate . . .

Heights, open water
Zayn X

Baked beans
Louis X

Snakes
Harry X

Hot spicy food
Liam X

Fake tan
Liam X

Olives
Harry X

Mayonnaise
Niall X

Spoons
Liam X

ONE DIRECTION3D

Any Direction

See if you can spot these words hidden in the grid opposite. They can run in . . . any direction!

HARRY STYLES
LIAM PAYNE
NIALL HORAN
ZAYN MALIK
LOUIS TOMLINSON

THE X FACTOR
ONE DIRECTION
SIMON COWELL
SYCO
FANS

FASHION
CONCERT
HAIR
UP ALL NIGHT
TAKE ME HOME

```
Q J D O J U E H K T M T D U L
Y O Z H A R R Y S T Y L E S J
L R X K A A E X Y R O O S Q Z
R O M S I I J J J E E Z I E A
S R U N Y L R Y Y C F E M E T
N G O I L M A U C N O F O N G
T X U T S B K M S O R E N O C
H A B U C T N W N C L C C I B
P Z N R L A O T A Y T B O T V
R I O U P R F M F C A Q W C O
A Y I F R T J X L Y P Z E E C
Y P H L X C S X E I E E L R Y
S N S J Y Q Q S O H N Z L I S
L I A M P A Y N E U T S K D O
J P F G W P N W Z E S O O E J
A X Z W Q I J D N T G H E N M
U P A L L N I G H T S J D O X
P I E D T A K E M E H O M E N
P G D V W X B I E Q W T S B P
C T N A R O H L L A I N U G O
```

37

Around the World

... in 176 concerts! One Direction are now global stars, and their second tour was selling out while they were still on the first one! Where could you see them?

Up All Night Tour
Dec 2011-July 2012

Watford, Westcliff-on-Sea, Wolverhampton, Manchester, Bournemouth, Birmingham, Plymouth, Nottingham, Brighton, London, Glasgow, Liverpool, Newcastle, Blackpool, Sheffield, Cardiff, London, Dublin, Belfast, Sydney, Melbourne, Brisbane, Auckland, Wellington, Uncasville, Fairfax, East Rutherford, New York City, Camden, Toronto, Detroit, Chicago, Mexico City, San Diego, Las Vegas, Phoenix, San Jose, Oakland, Los Angeles, Anaheim, Dallas, Houston, Atlanta, Charlotte, Tampa, Orlando, Fort Lauderdale.

Take Me Home Tour
February-November 2013

London, Glasgow, Cardiff, Dublin, Belfast, Dublin, Manchester, Liverpool, Sheffield, Nottingham, Birmingham, Liverpool, London, Newcastle, Glasgow, Sheffield, Birmingham, Manchester, Paris, Amnéville, Antwerp, Amsterdam, Oberhausen, Herning, Oslo, Stockholm, Copenhagen, Berlin, Hamburg, Zurich, Munich, Verona, Milan, Barcelona, Madrid, Lisbon, Mexico City, Fort Lauderdale, Miami, Louisville, Columbus, Nashville, Atlanta, Raleigh, Washington D.C., Philadelphia, Boston, Wantagh, East Rutherford, Montreal, Hershey, Pittsburgh, Toronto, Detroit, Tinley Park, Minneapolis, Kansas City, Houston, Dallas, Denver, Salt Lake City, Vancouver, Seattle, San Jose, Oakland, Las Vegas, San Diego, Los Angeles, Adelaide, Perth, Melbourne, Sydney, Christchurch, Auckland, Melbourne, Brisbane, Sydney, Melbourne, Japan.

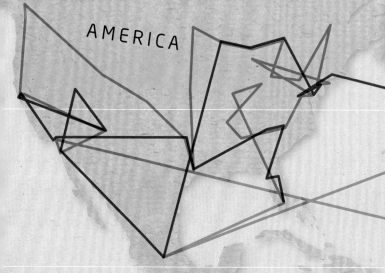

AMERICA

'This is Us', the 1D 3D movie, was shot during the Take Me Home Tour.

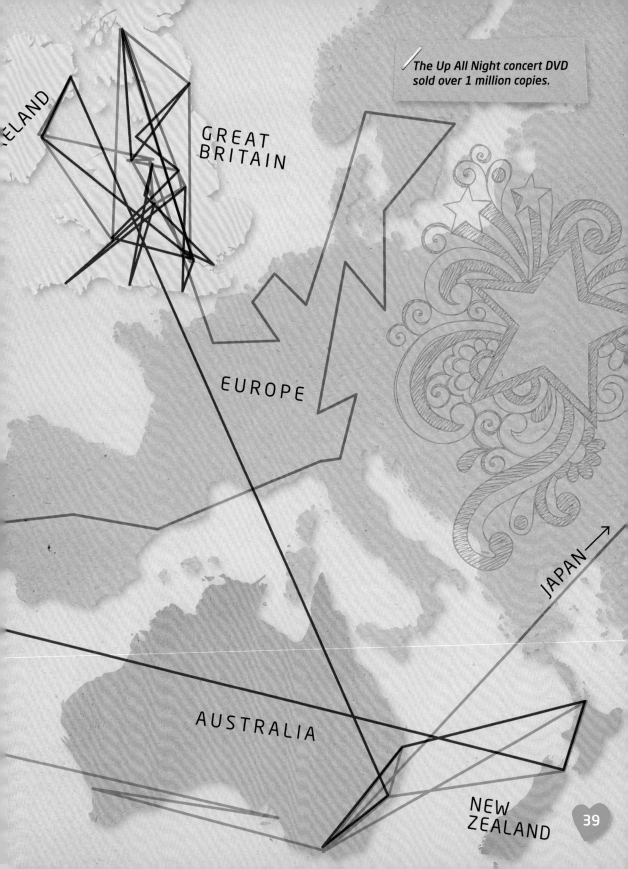

ELAND

GREAT
BRITAIN

EUROPE

JAPAN →

AUSTRALIA

NEW
ZEALAND

The Up All Night concert DVD
sold over 1 million copies.

Photo Funnies

These boys just can't stop joking. Write in what you think they're saying!

1D in Big Numbers

A few interesting facts – that you won't have seen this way!

guardian.co.uk/ barb.co.uk

ifpi.org

google.com 20 March 2013

The X Factor

The Final, part 1: 13.94 million viewers

The Final, part 2: 16.55 million viewers

Votes cast in Series 7: 15,488,019

Best-selling albums of 2012

Adele
21
8.3 million

Taylor Swift
Red
5.2 million

One Direction
Up All Night
4.5 million

One Direction
Take Me Home
4.4 million

Lana Del Ray
Born To Die
3.4 million

Google search results (millions)

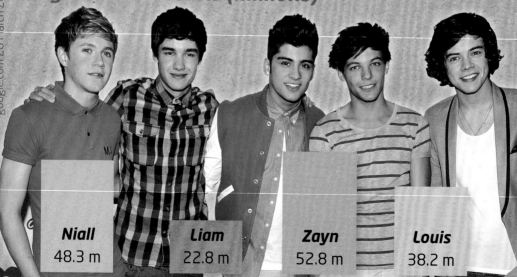

Niall
48.3 m

Liam
22.8 m

Zayn
52.8 m

Louis
38.2 m

Harry
189 m

Tour dates

X Factor Live Tour

Up All Night Tour

Take Me Home Tour

Solo time on Up All Night

- Niall
- Harry
- Liam
- Louis
- Zayn

Solo time on Take Me Home

- Niall
- Harry
- Liam
- Louis
- Zayn

Followers on Twitter

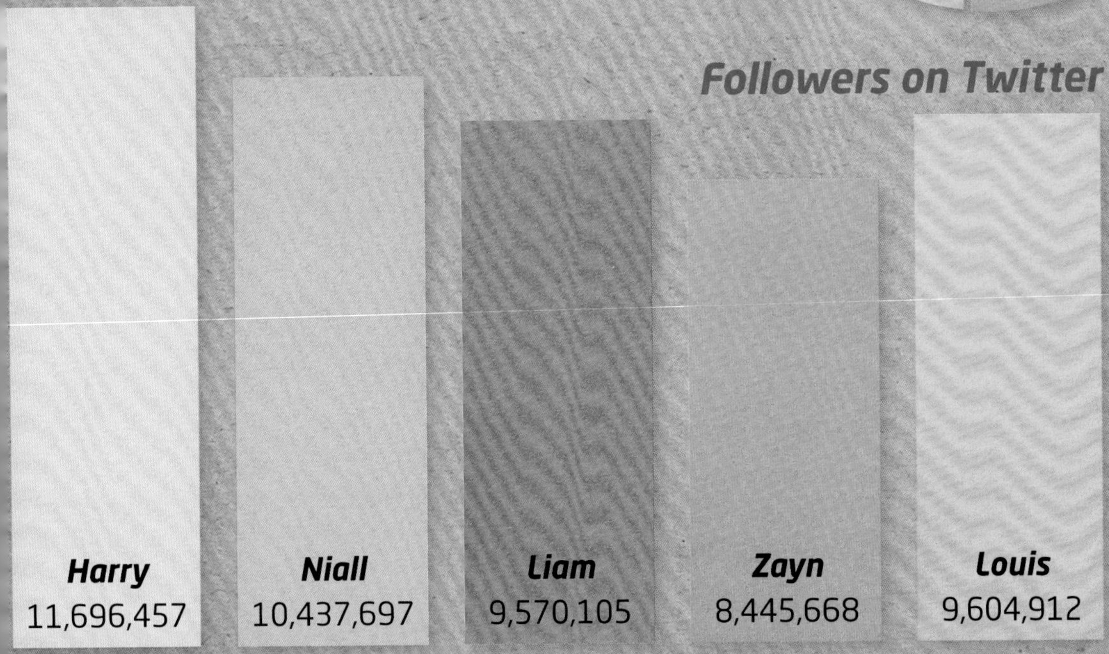

Harry	Niall	Liam	Zayn	Louis
11,696,457	10,437,697	9,570,105	8,445,668	9,604,912

twittercounter.com 20 March 2013

43

Best Band Ever?

One Direction aren't a 'boy band', they're boys in a band. How do they compare to other... boys in bands?

Take That

Gary Barlow, Howard Donald, Jason Orange, Mark Owen and Robbie Williams.

Formed 1990 in Manchester, England by Nigel Martin-Smith.

Albums *Take That and Party* (1992), *Everything Changes* (1993), *Nobody Else* (1995), *Beautiful World* (2006), *The* *Circus* (2008), *Progress* (2010)

Facts Take That were formed around the songwriting skills of Gary Barlow. They've sold over 45 million records, and their tours sell out faster than any other. They split up in 1996 after Robbie Williams left, and then reformed without him in 2006. He rejoined the band in 2010.

Backstreet Boys

AJ McLean, Howie Dorough, Nick Carter, Kevin Richardson and Brian Littrell.

Formed 1993 in Orlando, USA by Lou Pearlman.

Albums *Backstreet Boys* (1996), *Backstreet's Back* (1997), *Millennium* (1999), *Black & Blue* (2000), *Never* *Gone* (2005), *Unbreakable* (2007), *This Is Us* (2009).

Facts BSB have sold over 130 million records, making them one of the world's best-selling groups. They took a break for a couple of years from 2002, and became a quartet in 2006 when Kevin Richardson left. He's now rejoined the group - they are working on a new album.

*NSYNC

Chris Kirkpatrick, Justin Timberlake, JC Chasez, Joey Fatone and Lance Bass.

Formed 1995 in Orlando, USA by Lou Pearlman.

Albums *NSYNC* (1997), *Home for Christmas* (1998), *No Strings Attached* (2000), *Celebrity* (2001).

Facts Chris Kirkpatrick tried to get into the Backstreet Boys before he helped set up *NSYNC. Justin Timberlake and JC Chasez were both in the Micky Mouse Club on TV before they joined the band. They sold over 50 million albums before retiring in 2002. Justin Timberlake has been busy ever since!

Westlife

Nicky Byrne, Kian Egan, Mark Feehily, Shane Filan and Brian McFadden.

Formed 1998 in Sligo, Ireland by Louis Walsh and Simon Cowell.

Albums *Westlife* (1999), *Coast to Coast* (2000), *World of Our Own* (2001), *Turnaround* (2003), *...Allow Us To Be Frank* (2004), *Face to Face* (2005), *The Love Album* (2006), *Back Home* (2007), *Where We Are* (2009), *Gravity* (2010).

Facts Westlife were hugely successful everywhere – except America. They sold over 44 million albums and had 14 number one songs. Brian left the band in 2004, while the others continued as a quartet until they finally quit in 2011.

The Wanted

Max George, Nathan Sykes, Tom Parker, Jay McGuinness and Siva Kaneswaran.

Formed 2009 in London by Jayne Collins.

Albums *The Wanted* (2010), *Battleground* (2011), *Third Strike* (2013).

Facts Max and Tom both auditioned for *The X Factor* before joining The Wanted. They've had number one singles in the UK and Ireland, and recorded the 2011 Comic Relief single. They've said they'll be in their own US reality TV show in 2013.

Union J

Josh Cuthbert, JJ (Jamie) Hamblett, Jaymi Hensley and George Shelley.

Formed 2012 in London.

Albums None. Their debut single should be released in June 2013.

Facts Just like 1D, Union J were formed on *The X Factor*. They dominated the online gossip about the 2012 series, and only just missed out on making it to the final. It's early days, but there's a lot of good feeling around these guys. Should 1D be nervous?

Welcome to Fanworld!

Right from the start, 1D have had the best fans in the world. They make signs and clothes and gifts, they talk and post online all the time, and they gather in huge crowds to cheer and scream every time the boys appear in public. Directioners have in-jokes they only use with each other. If you know what 'Do you ship Larry?' means, we're talking about you!

▲ Pretending to be fans in November 2010.

America

'It's incredible to have people show their support when you're doing something you love.'
Harry

48

Mexico

Japan

Australia

'So crazy to think that we have only known each other 2 years. It's been so amazing and we have got to do so many amazing things all thanks to each and every one of you guys. It's all gone by so quickly but I'm sure we will have many many more times to come.'
One Direction Facebook post

49

One Way or Another

1D have their hearts in the right places – they're happy to help a good cause

Right from the start One Direction have done great work for charity. They appeared on two of the *X Factor* charity singles, and they also sang on the Children in Need fundraising show two years in a row. But 2013 saw their biggest effort yet. They were asked to record the official Comic Relief single, 'One Way or Another (Teenage Kicks)', and were taken to Africa to see how Red Nose Day cash changes lives.

The group visited projects in Ghana, and met the people whose lives have been turned around as a result. They were very moved by what they saw, and were determined to do all they could to help with the single. They recorded the video themselves, to save costs, and donated all their royalties and profits to the charity. They even auctioned off the clothes they wore in Ghana, raising a massive £11,000.

The single shot straight to number one in Britain, and reached number one in an amazing 63 countries – that's really fantastic work, guys!

They were also asked their favourite cheesy jokes . . . sorry, these are terrible!

Red Nose Day raised over £75 million in 2013 – the best ever result!

The BEST!

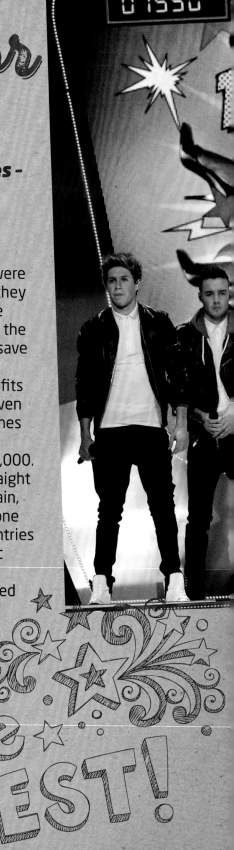

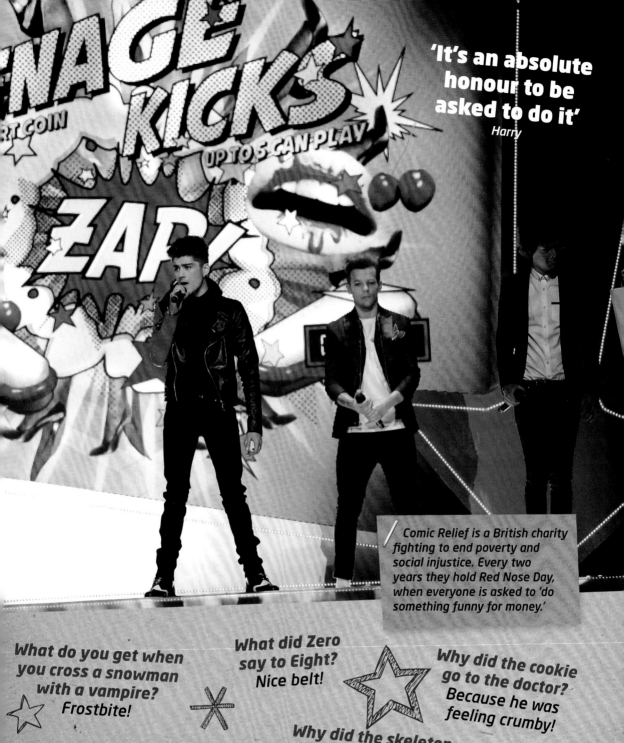

'It's an absolute honour to be asked to do it'
Harry

Comic Relief is a British charity fighting to end poverty and social injustice. Every two years they hold Red Nose Day, when everyone is asked to 'do something funny for money.'

What do you get when you cross a snowman with a vampire?
Frostbite!

What did Zero say to Eight?
Nice belt!

Why did the cookie go to the doctor?
Because he was feeling crumby!

What do you get when you cross a pig and a cactus?
A porky-pine!

Why did the skeleton go to the movies by himself?
He had no body to go with him!

On the Red Carpet

The boys have smartened up a lot since *The X Factor*. Success means there's cool stuff for them to try on all the time, and probably someone to help with the ironing! Here are the defining features of the 1D look:

- Show off your forearms
- Skinny peg leg trousers
- Stripes (Louis only)
- Flawless hair
- Bit of stubble
- Everything clean and ironed
- Accessorize carefully
- Can't go wrong with a tight jacket
- Dress for the occasion
- Red, white and blue . . .
- . . . or black. Sorted!
- Love those high street labels
- Only Harry can get away with a bowtie!
- No socks for Louis
- Co-ordinating, not matching

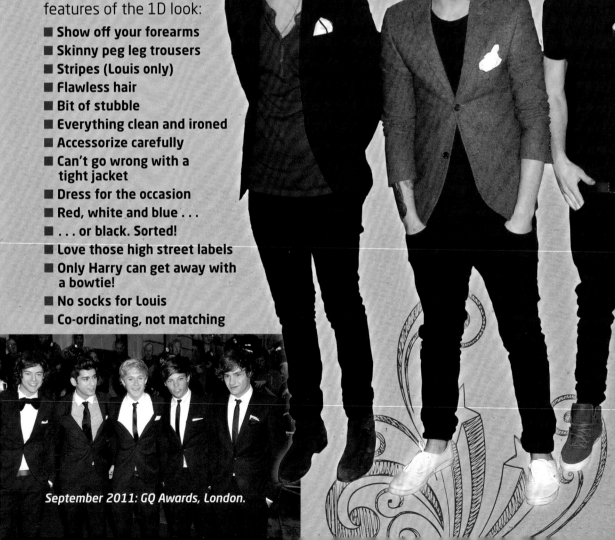

September 2011: GQ Awards, London.

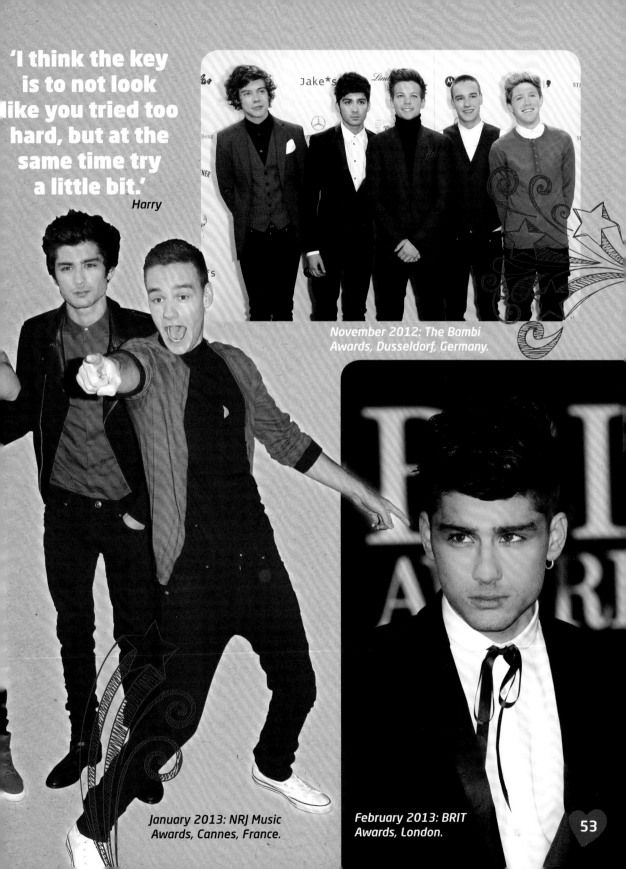

'I think the key is to not look like you tried too hard, but at the same time try a little bit.'

Harry

November 2012: The Bambi Awards, Dusseldorf, Germany.

January 2013: NRJ Music Awards, Cannes, France.

February 2013: BRIT Awards, London.

53

On the Red Carpet

February 2013: BRIT Awards, London.

Jingle Bell Ball

Fave labels

Everyday
Jack Wills
Urban Outfitters
Superdry
River Island
A.P.C.
Lazy Oaf
Abercrombie & Fitch

Smart
Topman
ASOS
Alexander McQueen
Burberry Prorsum
Commes Des Garcons

Footwear
Converse
TOMS (Louis)
Nike
Vans

Liam in a cardigan designed by Alexander McQueen - smooth!

February 2012: BRIT Awards, London.

September 2012: MTV
Video Music Awards,
Los Angeles.

'I like fashion. When I look
back at the kind of stuff
I wore on *The X Factor*,
I laugh. There's no excuse.'

Harry

Onesies during X Factor: a look
they wouldn't wear now!

One Big Quiz

04 Whose One Direction doll is tallest?

01 Whose birthday is nearest to Christmas?

05 What are the names of Zayn's sisters?

02 What was the name of Harry's band at school?

06 What was Harry's pet hamster called?

03 Who grew up the furthest north?

07 Who was on *The X Factor* first?

08 What is the name of Niall's brother?

09 Who is the only band member to call Harry 'Hazza'?

10 They once gave Simon Cowell a birthday card with money in it . . . How much money?

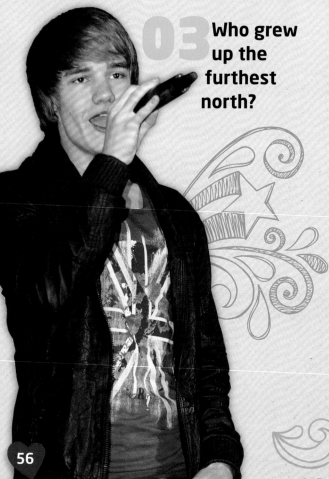

11 Which football club does Niall support?

12 Which song did Ed Sheeran write on One Direction's second album?

13 Which *X Factor* contestant supported 1D on their first tour?

14 What is the name of the online 1D cartoon by animator Mark Parsons?

15 What role did Louis play in his school production of *Grease*?

16 What is the only book Niall says he's read all the way through?

17 What song did Harry audition with on *The X Factor*?

18 What nickname did Liam's sisters give him when he was younger?

19 Who dressed up in a fat suit for a video and asked for hugs?

20 On whose hairy leg did Harry shave his initials?

love you

1D: A to Z!

▼ Where's your hat, Matt?

A **Auditions** - luckily they all made it through in the same year

B **Belle Amie** - formed at boot camp along with 1D

C **Carrots** - Louis isn't that fond of them at all

D **Daddy Direction** - aka Liam, as he tries to keep them on track

E **Eldest** - the one who acts pretty childish sometimes

F **Fans** - they're not crazy, they're passionate!

G **Glasses** - Louis needs them, and Zayn wears them pretty often

H **Harry's Hair** - the most famous mop in the world

I **Ireland** - the reason Liam's accent is so attractive!

J **Judge's House** - where it became clear this band might work after all

K **Kids in America** - the boys sang this in Week Five

L **Larry, Lilo and Lirry** - just some of the ways fans pair up the boys

M **Matt Cardle** - beat 1D to the top spot, but stayed friends with the lads

N **NO Jimmy protested!** - do you know what it means?

O **Olympics** - they sang at the closing ceremony in 2012

P **Practical Jokes** - watch out when you're sleeping, anything could happen!

Q **Queen** - 1D performed for Her Majesty at the Royal Variety Performance

R **Rebecca Ferguson** - got second place above 1D and dated Zayn for a few months

S **Shops** - there's a 1D World in Sydney, Brisbane, Toronto, Vancouver, Chicago and Stockholm

T **Tattoos** - only Niall hasn't been inked . . . yet

U **Up All Night** - the third best-selling album in the world for 2012

V **Vas Happenin?** - Zayn's favourite phrase

W **What Makes You Beautiful** - the fab first single

X **X Factor** - where it all began for our favourite five

Y **Youngest** - the one who seems to prefer older women

Z **Zayn** - the tidy one!

ANSWERS

Spot the Difference (p.28)

Any Direction (p.36)

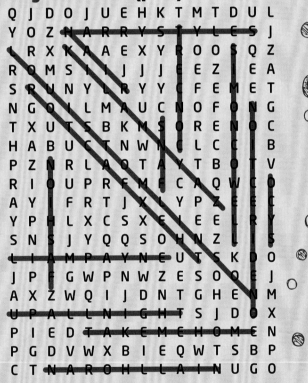

```
Q J D O J U E H K T M T D U L
Y O Z H A R R Y S T Y L E S J
L R X X A E X Y R O O S Q Z
R O M S I I J J E E Z I E A
S P U N Y L R Y Y C F E M E T
N G O I L M A U C N O F O N G
T X U T S B K M S O R E N O C
H A B U C T N W N C L C C I B
P Z N R L A O T A Y T B O T V
R I O U P R F M F C A Q W C D
A Y I F R T J X L Y P Z E E I
Y P H L X C S X E E E L R Y
S N S J Y Q Q S O H N Z I I S
L I A M P A Y N E U T S K D O
J P F G W P N W Z E S O O E J
A X Z W Q I J D N T G H E N M
U P A L L N I G H T S J D O X
P I E D T A K E M E H O M E N
P G D V W X B I E Q W T S B P
C T N A R O H L L A I N U G O
```

One Big Quiz (p.56)

01: Louis. 02: White Eskimo. 03: Zayn, in Bradford. 04: They're all meant to be the same size, but isn't the Niall doll a bit taller? 05: Doniya, Waliyha and Safaa. 06: Hamster. 07: Liam, in 2008. 08: Greg. 09: Liam. 10: £2.50 – 50p each. 11: Derby County. 12: 'Little Things'. 13: Olly Murs. 14: The Adventurous Adventures of One Direction. 15: Danny Zuko. 16: *To Kill A Mockingbird*. 17: 'Isn't She Lovely' by Stevie Wonder. 18: Cheesy Head. 19: Louis. 20: Zayn.

▲ Sophia, Rebecca and Esther from Belle Amie in 2011.